A TRUE BOOK™

The Undersea World

TAMRA B. ORR

Children's Press®
An Imprint of Scholastic Inc.

Content Consultant

Annie Mercier, PhD, Associate Professor,
Department of Ocean Sciences, Memorial University,
Newfoundland and Labrador, Canada

Library of Congress Cataloging-in-Publication Data

Names: Orr, Tamra, author.

Title: The undersea world / by Tamra B. Orr.

Other titles: True book.

Description: New York : Children's Press, an imprint of Scholastic Inc., [2017] I Series: A true book I Includes bibliographical references and index.

Identifiers: LCCN 2015048497I ISBN 9780531218594 (library binding) I ISBN 9780531227770 (pbk.)

Subjects: LCSH: Ocean—Juvenile literature. I Oceanography—Juvenile literature. I Underwater exploration—Juvenile literature.

Classification: LCC GC85 .O77 2017 I DDC 551.46—dc23

LC record available at http://lccn.loc.gov/2015048497

© 2017 Scholastic Inc.

All rights reserved. Published in 2017 by Children's Press, an imprint of Scholastic Inc.

Printed in China 62

SCHOLASTIC, CHILDREN'S PRESS, A TRUE BOOK™, and associated logos are trademarks and/or registered trademarks of Scholastic Inc.

1 2 3 4 5 6 7 8 9 10 R 26 25 24 23 22 21 20 19 18 17

Front cover: An Exosuit in the ocean

Back cover: A tiger shark and diver off the coast of Australia

TRUE BOOK™

The Undersea World

The Exosuit allows a diver to explore as deep as 1,000 feet (305 meters) under the ocean surface.

TAMRA B. ORR

SCHOLASTIC

Find the Truth!

Everything you are about to read is true *except* for one of the sentences on this page.

Which one is **TRUE**?

T or F Experts have explored about 5 percent of the undersea world.

T or F The deepest parts of the ocean are too dark and cold for any creatures to live there.

Find the answers in this book.

Contents

THE **BIG** TRUTH!

California bigeye
octopus

Sunken ship

Yonaguni
Monument

Maps generally divide the global ocean into the Pacific, Atlantic, Indian, Arctic, and Southern Oceans.

A World of Water

From space, Earth appears as a round planet with a few spots of brown and many areas of blue. All of that blue is water. Water covers about three-fourths of Earth's surface. Most of it is found in an area called the **global ocean**.

There is a lot to explore in all that water. People have found shipwrecks from centuries ago. They have seen some of the world's strangest creatures. They have also found man-made structures—even ancient palaces and temples!

Undiscovered Wonders

As much as explorers have found under the water's surface, there is far more that has not been found. Experts estimate we have explored only about 5 percent of the global ocean. While people have created maps of parts of the ocean's floor, they are not very detailed. There are also wide areas of the ocean floor that have not been explored at all.

Shipwrecks, new animal species, and more are waiting to be found in the unexplored parts of the ocean.

Air tanks and other diving equipment help people explore the upper levels of the ocean.

Why has so little ocean exploration been done? First, the undersea world is very vast. Second, it takes special equipment to explore underwater. Experienced divers cannot go deeper than a few hundred feet without risking their lives. Scuba tanks, which contain breathable air, allow divers to travel deeper and stay under longer. But water pressure, or the weight of the water above them, makes it impossible to go very deep.

To help people explore the ocean's deeper levels, experts use vessels called submersibles that dive underwater like submarines. Most submersibles are unmanned. Others have large windows and bright lights so passengers can see in the darkness. They often have cameras attached so they can take pictures. Many new submersibles have built-in robot arms for reaching out and taking samples. All of this equipment, however, is expensive!

A robotic arm reaches out from a submersible to retrieve an artifact from a shipwreck.

In the photic zone, the sun's rays shine down through the water.

The Ocean Zones

The top layer of water is warmed by the rays of the sun. This is the sunlit, or photic, zone. The sunlit zone extends from the surface down to about 650 feet (198 meters). It is where most of the world's familiar, brightly colored sea creatures live, including corals, reef fish, and sea stars. You'll also find sharks, turtles, dolphins, and sea horses.

The twilight, or disphotic, zone extends to about 3,200 feet (975 m). It is darker and colder than the sunlit zone above it. Even so, the seafloor in this zone is often teeming with life. You might find octopuses or even giant sea spiders. Less wildlife lives in the twilight zone's open ocean. Animals there include giant squids and sperm whales. Some creatures are **bioluminescent**. The light may attract prey, confuse predators, or help locate mates.

Sperm whales sometimes spend time in the open ocean in the twilight zone.

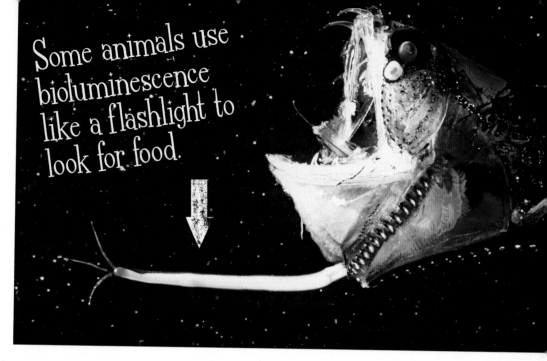

Some animals use bioluminescence like a flashlight to look for food.

Deep-sea dragonfish

Below the twilight zone is the midnight, or aphotic, zone. This zone reaches down to the very bottom of the ocean. In some places, the zone extends about 7 miles (11 kilometers) below the ocean surface. There is no light here. Some of the creatures at this level are so bizarre that people sometimes describe them as "monsters." These deep-sea animals include the anglerfish, gulper eel, and flapjack devilfish.

The California bigeye octopus
is one of many octopus
species found in the twilight or
midnight zones.

Life in the Ocean

Quick! Name five ocean creatures. Many people may say whales, sharks, dolphins, jellyfish, and octopuses. The ocean's sunlit layer is full of such **species**. The sea actually contains more than a million species of plants and animals. Only a fraction of them have been identified, and most of those live in the bright and bustling upper waters.

The biggest deep-sea octopus ever found was 59 feet (18 m) long.

Coral

Tiny creatures called coral thrive in the sunlit layer. Corals grow on top of each other, and their skeletons build up over time to form coral reefs. These reefs come in all colors of the rainbow. The long, thin fingers of red sea whip coral are found in shallow water. Orange sun coral looks like a garden of bright flowers inside caves. Coral reefs are home to so many different species that they are sometimes compared to rain forests.

Coral reefs are slowly being destroyed by pollution and too much fishing.

Creatures of the Deep

One of the strangest life-forms that we find past the bright photic zone is the blobfish. It has almost no bones or muscles. It floats thousands of feet below the ocean surface. The

The yeti crab's claws and legs look like they are covered in feathers or hair.

rare frilled shark looks like an eel but has 25 rows of razor-sharp teeth like a shark. The yeti crab lives more than 7,000 feet (2,134 m) down. The featherlike hairs on its claws help the blind creature find food and avoid obstacles.

The Ocean's Forests

Although seaweed is as widespread as many land-based weeds, the term *weed* is not accurate for seaweed. Weeds are usually unwanted plants, and seaweed is something every ocean needs. These **algae** vary in size, from so tiny you need a microscope to see them to hundreds of feet long. Some larger species grow in clusters to create underwater forests. Seaweed comes in many colors, including red, green, brown, and black.

Viewed from underwater, seaweed forests look much like the forests that grow on land.

Some types of seaweed float freely in the water, while others root themselves in one spot on the ground. Seaweed is a place for marine species to hide and live. It also provides food for many creatures. Even people enjoy eating seaweed as part of their diets. Kelp is a type of seaweed that is high in vitamins, minerals, and fiber. It is often used in a Japanese food called sushi.

Sea turtles are among the many animals that rely on seaweed as a source of food.

Governments and organizations around the world are developing methods of sustainable fishing.

Humans and Ocean Life

Ocean organisms have a huge impact on humans. Fish and shellfish form about 16 percent of the world's meat and other protein foods. Millions of people also travel to see marine ecosystems up close. This creates jobs and brings money into the local economy.

However, these activities also cause harm. Overfishing reduces fish populations and destroys the ecosystems where they live. Tourists may leave behind garbage or accidentally hurt animals, coral reefs, or other ocean life.

Ocean Explorer

Jacques Cousteau (1910–1997) was an explorer, inventor, and filmmaker who was fascinated by water. His love of the undersea world was so strong he wanted to share it with everyone. On his ship, *Calypso*, he sailed the world. He filmed his adventures and put the films on television. Cousteau also invented the Aqua-Lung for breathing underwater. He created the first underwater habitats for humans. His life was dedicated to the ocean.

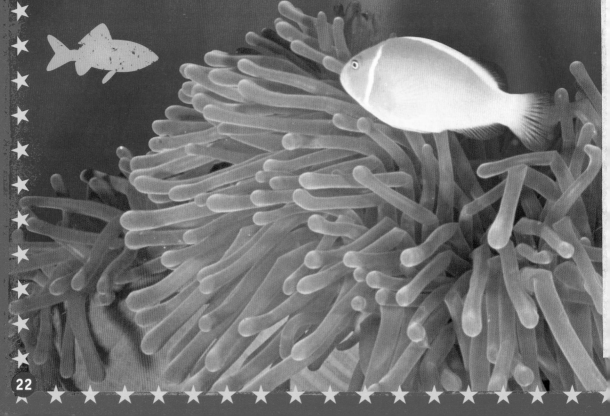

Sea Lights

The ocean is filled with lights, which serve a range of purposes. Here are just a few examples of what light can do in the world's waters.

FINDING FOOD

Unlike most deep-sea fish, the smalltooth dragonfish can see the color red. It produces its own red light, which it uses to spot prey. The unsuspecting creatures don't see the attacker coming.

HIDING

The hatchetfish lights its body to mimic the sunlight streaming through the water's surface. A predator swimming below could look up and not notice a thing. That keeps it alive!

ALARM

If the environment is just right, certain types of tiny ocean creatures called plankton light up. At night, waves crashing onto shore glow blue. The light is meant to startle a predator, hopefully making it stop eating. The light also attracts other, larger predators. These animals don't eat the plankton, but they might make a meal of the plankton's attacker.

Exploring shipwrecks is like stepping—or swimming—back in time.

Shipwrecks and Treasures

"Amazing Shipwreck Found at Last!"

"Lost Ship Discovered in the Ocean!"

"Treasure Chests of Gold Coins Located in the Deep"

Have you ever seen headlines like these? Stories of amazing shipwrecks and the incredible treasures they hold are often in the news. It's no wonder these stories keep popping up. The United Nations estimates there are more than three million shipwrecks under the world's waters.

Lost at Sea

Some of these ships were lost during storms. Others ran into some kind of trouble, such as the RMS *Titanic* hitting an iceberg in 1912. Others were destroyed during battle. However they ended up there, shipwrecks and the cargo they carried tempt explorers of all kinds. People from archaeologists to treasure seekers have long searched the deep for these riches.

The RMS *Titanic* carried mail as well as people. RMS stands for Royal Mail Service.

Sunken ships can support the local ecosystem, providing a home for sea creatures.

Sunken Treasures

Some shipwrecks contain highly valuable items. The *Nuestra Señora de las Mercedes* was an early 19th century Spanish Navy ship. It carried coins worth $500 million today. A treasure-seeking company found it off the coast of Portugal in 2007.

Another ship, the *Nuestra Señora de Atocha*, was crossing the Florida Keys in 1622. It was full of gold, copper, silver, and jewels. A hurricane sank the ship. It was found in 1985, its cargo worth an estimated $450 million.

The Spanish government fought for ownership of the coins and other treasures found on the *Nuestra Señora de las Mercedes*.

Some shipwrecks are ancient. Recently, explorers found 22 wrecks more than 2,500 years old near a group of Greek islands. Other wrecks are pirate ships, such as the *Whydah Gally* found in 1984. Captain "Black Sam" Bellamy's sunken ship contained 200,000 **artifacts** worth $400 million. Military ships also litter ocean floors. In 1941, a German U-boat torpedoed a British Treasury ship full of silver. It sank and was not discovered until 2012.

The *Uluburun* shipwreck, discovered in the Mediterranean Sea, is one of the oldest ever found.

Today, ships are designed to be much stronger. However, wrecks still occur. In 1975, the SS *Edmund Fitzgerald* was crossing Lake Superior toward Michigan. It encountered a storm with powerful winds, high waves, and freezing temperatures. The ship sank 17 miles (27 km) away from shore.

Shipwrecks often contain more than coins and jewels. Divers find pottery, glass, dishes, and even foods and drinks in the watery depths.

A photograph taken by explorers shows the wreck of the *Edmund Fitzgerald* at the bottom of Lake Superior.

A diver sits on a truck that sank with a ship in the Red Sea near Egypt.

Finders Keepers?

Who owns treasures found underwater? People have long debated the answer. Much depends on the wreck's location. In 1987, the United States passed a law giving state governments the right to claim anything found within 3 nautical miles (5.6 km) of their coastline. Most other countries have similar laws. If a wreck is found within a country's territory, the treasures belong to that country. They do not belong to the people who found them.

A Great Explorer

Oceanographer Robert Ballard always knew what he wanted to be. "From a very early age, . . . I wanted to explore the ocean floor," he said. In 1985, he found the wreck of the famous RMS *Titanic*. In Ballard's lifetime, he has gone on 135 **expeditions**. He has found everything from previously unknown life-forms to ancient shipwrecks. When asked what his most important discovery is, he replies, "The one I'm about to make."

Relics and Ruins

More than 130 feet (40 m) down in China's Qiandao Lake is Shi Cheng, or the Lion City. This ancient city has been on the lake's bottom for roughly 60 years. People built the city between 25 and 200 CE. In 1959, engineers created Qiandao Lake when building a new dam in the area. The Lion City was submerged. Divers, however, can still visit the city's temples and lion statues.

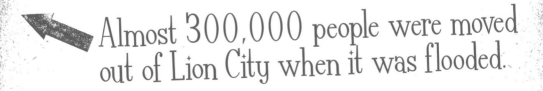

Almost 300,000 people were moved out of Lion City when it was flooded.

Researchers have found temples and burial chambers underwater that are hundreds or thousands of years old.

A Glimpse at the Past

Most underwater ruins date back hundreds and even thousands of years. In southern Greece, an ancient village known as Pavlopetri sits under 13 feet (4 m) of water. Its 9 acres (3.6 hectares) feature more than a dozen buildings, as well as roads and a cemetery. The city is more than 5,000 years old, making it one of the world's oldest known submerged cities. Experts believe it sank because of an earthquake around 1000 BCE.

Finding Cleopatra

Marine archaeologist Franck Goddio was working off the coast of Alexandria in Egypt in the mid-1990s. Goddio had been exploring this underwater area for more than 20 years. Already, he and his team had found golden coins, statues, and vessels. Many had the image of Cleopatra, Egypt's famous queen, on them. Could her lost palace be here, too?

Franck Goddio shows off an ancient Egyptian statue that he helped uncover.

Cleopatra's palace and temple sank between the 4th and 8th centuries CE because of earthquakes and **tsunamis**. The buildings remained lost for more than 1,600 years. Goddio and his team finally uncovered the palace in 1996. Through the years, they have found everything from huge statues to sphinxes. Almost all of the artifacts are completely intact because they have been covered in sediment. This protected them from the damage of salt water.

Timeline of Undersea Innovation

1868
Charles Wyville Thomson discovers sea life at 14,400 feet (4,389 m).

1943
Jacques Cousteau invents the Aqua-Lung, allowing people to breathe underwater.

Smaller Treasures

Many of the amazing treasures found underwater are small but important. Divers have found lamps, tools, teacups, ceramic jugs, wine bottles, and glass bowls. In June 2013, scientists analyzed the contents of some sealed drug containers found on a 2,000-year-old sunken cargo ship. Inside were unharmed pills. The pills contained zinc, starch, beeswax, and a number of materials taken from plants. Such information provides a peek at life thousands of years ago.

1960
Scientists explore the Mariana Trench, Earth's deepest location, for the first time.

1985
Robert Ballard discovers the wreck of the *Titanic*.

37

The Yonaguni Monument
dates back at least
5,000 years.

Pyramids, Circles, and Laboratories

Cities and shipwrecks, temples and roads—what else has been found deep below the water's surface?

In 1986, a tour guide found some tall, rectangular-shaped rock formations in the waters off Japan's southern islands. The structure became known as the Yonaguni Monument, named after the nearby island Yonaguni Jima. No one is sure what the rocks are. For years, experts have debated whether these oddly shaped rocks were created by nature or by people.

Understanding Yonaguni

The Yonaguni Monument looks like ancient pyramids, complete with steps to the top. The rocks are surrounded by what appear to be temples and a castle, all connected by roads. Some experts claim years of wave **erosion** created these pyramids.

Others disagree. They point to markings that may be drawings on the side of the Yonaguni Monument.

Researchers point out large holes in the Yonaguni Monument.

The amazing designs created by puffer fish look like works of art.

Circles in the Sand

For more than 10 years, the beautiful circles found on the ocean floor off the coast of Japan baffled divers. What—or who—creates these designs? Amazingly, a certain type of puffer fish makes them. The male puffer fish moves its fins just right to shift the sand on the seafloor and create the intricate designs. Although the fish are only 5 inches (12.7 centimeters) long, the circles they make are 7 feet (2 m) in diameter.

A male and female puffer fish join together to mate in the male's circular nest.

Why do puffer fish work so hard on these circles? To get the girl, of course! Female puffer fish look at the circles and, if they like a design, they mate with its creator. It is unclear what the females are looking for in these designs or what makes one better than another. Experts do know that females lay their eggs in the design's middle. Then they leave, knowing the males will stay to guard the eggs.

Pushing the Boundaries

Is it better to explore outer space or undersea? While both environments are important, some experts argue ocean exploration should be the priority. Climate change and its effect on the ocean is a focus of projects like the Aquarius Underwater Laboratory in the Florida Keys. Ocean exploration might also lead to solutions for everything from illness to protection against natural disasters.

Who knows what amazing answers still wait just underneath the water's surface? ★

The Aquarius Underwater Laboratory sits 60 feet (18 m) under the ocean's surface.

True Statistics

Percent of Earth's water that is salt water: About 97

Percent of Earth's water that is found in glaciers and ice caps: Between 2 and 3

Estimated number of aquatic (water) species that experts have found and named: Approximately 1.5 million

Estimated number of aquatic species that have not yet been discovered: More than 50 million

Percent of international trade that is carried by ships: About 90

Percent of international communications that rely on underwater cables: Nearly 50

Percent of ocean waters that are considered to be "deep sea": About 90

Speed of sound in water compared to speed of sound in air: Nearly five times faster in water

Did you find the truth?

 Experts have explored about 5 percent of the undersea world.

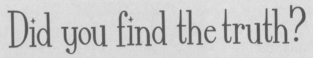 The deepest parts of the ocean are too dark and cold for any creatures to live there.

Resources

Books

Hague, Bradley. *Alien Deep: Revealing the Mysterious Living World at the Bottom of the Ocean*. Washington, DC: National Geographic, 2012.

Nemeth, Jason D. *Rivers, Lakes, and Oceans*. New York: PowerKids Press, 2012.

Reynolds, Toby, and Paul Calver. *Ocean Life*. Hauppauge, NY: Barron's Educational Series, Inc., 2015.

Visit this Scholastic Web site for more information on the undersea world:
★ www.factsfornow.scholastic.com
Enter the keywords **Undersea World**

Important Words

algae (AL-jee) small plants without roots or stems that grow mainly in water

artifacts (AHR-tuh-fakts) objects made or changed by human beings, especially a tool or weapon used in the past

bioluminescent (by-oh-loo-mih-NESS-uhnt) able to naturally produce light

erosion (i-ROH-zhuhn) the wearing away of rock, soil, or other material by wind and water over time

expeditions (ek-spuh-DISH-uhnz) long trips made for a specific purpose

global ocean (GLOH-buhl OH-shuhn) Earth's single, continuous ocean; often divided into several separately named oceans on maps

oceanographer (oh-shuh-NAH-gruh-fur) an expert who studies the life and natural processes associated with the ocean

species (SPEE-sheez) one of the groups into which animals and plants of the same genus are divided

tsunamis (tsoo-NAH-meez) large ocean waves caused by an earthquake or volcano

Index

Page numbers in **bold** indicate illustrations.

About the Author

Tamra Orr is the author of hundreds of books for readers of all ages. She has a degree in English and secondary education from Ball State University, and now lives in the Pacific Northwest. She is the mother of four children, and loves to spend her free time reading, writing, and going camping. She loves nothing more than camping near the Oregon coastline so she can listen, watch, and appreciate the endless ocean waves.